parenting
with hope

STUDY GUIDE

MELISSA B. KRUGER

Eph. 3:14-21
Pray Every Morning

HARVEST HOUSE PUBLISHERS
EUGENE, OREGON

Published in association with the literary agency of Wolgemuth & Wilson.

Cover design by Faceout Studio, Tim Green

Interior design by Janelle Coury

For bulk, special sales, or ministry purchases, please call 1-800-547-8979.
Email: Customerservice@hhpbooks.com

This logo is a federally registered trademark of the Hawkins Children's LLC. Harvest House Publishers, Inc., is the exclusive licensee of this trademark.

Parenting with Hope Study Guide

Copyright © 2024 by Melissa B. Kruger
Published by Harvest House Publishers
Eugene, Oregon 97408
www.harvesthousepublishers.com

ISBN 978-0-7369-8804-9 (pbk)
ISBN 978-0-7369-8805-6 (eBook)

Printed in the United States of America

24 25 26 27 28 29 30 31 32 / BP / 10 9 8 7 6 5 4 3 2 1

Contents

Part 4: Group Discussion Questions

How to Use This Study Guide

I f you're like me, you would welcome a parenting instruction manual, especially during the teen years. I'd love for someone to whisper in my ear, guide me in wisdom, and say, "Do this!" and "Don't do that!" Every day, we have parenting decisions to make and it's difficult to know whether we're choosing what's best. We're learning at each stage of the journey. Parenting is a lot like trying to build a car while driving it.

While we don't have a ready resource manual for all our decisions, thankfully, we have help. The Holy Spirit is available to guide us in supernatural ways with wisdom and insight. Jesus promised his disciples, "When the Spirit of truth comes, he will guide you into all the truth" (John 16:13).

I hope this study guide will allow you time to slow down and listen to the Spirit. As we read various Bible passages, God's Word transforms us: reminding us of God's goodness, convicting us of truth, nourishing our souls, and providing wisdom. As you spend time in prayer, God will be at work in both you and your teen. These moments spent in quietness and reflection will fortify and strengthen you for the busiest moments of your day.

To help you glean as much as possible, the study guide will

follow this pattern: **Read** the chapter, **Respond** to a few questions about the chapter, **Reflect** upon various Bible passages, and **Request** to the Lord through prayer.

As you use this guide, begin by reading the corresponding chapter in *Parenting with Hope*. Take notes, underline, and write in the margins. I'll ask three questions so you can begin responding to what you've read. Don't skip this section! Taking the time to write out your answers is a key part of remembering what you're reading. As you thoughtfully engage with what you've read, you're more likely to recall these principles in the midst of daily parenting struggles.

In addition, I'll guide you through some Bible passages and questions so that you have time to meditate and reflect upon the Word on your own. You can do all of these in one sitting, or spend a couple of days working through them. You don't have to write out your answers (no one is checking your homework). However, the more you write out, the more you will remember. To help close your time in prayer, I've left some space for you to consider how to pray and provided a Bible verse to help guide you in prayer. As you read the book and use this guide, I hope you'll be able to see God at work in specific ways in response to your prayers.

In Part 4 of this study guide are **Group Discussion Questions** (from page 95 onward) for each of the lessons. If you are reading the book *Parenting with Hope* with others, then you can go through these questions with your spouse, a group of moms, a group of dads, or perhaps a couple's small group or Sunday school class. So when you finish the **Read**, **Respond**, **Reflect**, and **Request** questions in each lesson, make sure to go on to the **Group Discussion Questions** for that same lesson in the group discussion section. Talking about these ideas in community will be such a rich blessing.

As you study, I'm praying for you:

> *May the Spirit direct your steps and guide you on your path. May the Word give wisdom, insight, and clarity. May God remind you daily of his grace through Jesus. May you experience his presence and know he's with you during this journey. Amen.*

Let's begin.

PART 1

The Basics: Foundations of a Christian Home

An Instruction Manual for Life: God's Word

Your testimonies are my delight; they are my counselors (Psalm 119:24).

Read

In your copy of *Parenting with Hope*, read chapter 1, "The Instruction Manual for Life: God's Word," and then take a moment to write down your responses to the questions below.

Respond

- What biblical principles stood out to you in this chapter?

  - Revival, refreshment, wisdom, joy, + enlightenment are found in God's Word
  - There's no other way to bear fruit except abiding in Jesus - apart from Him we can do nothing.
  - Only Jesus can secure our contentment.

- In what ways did this chapter impact how you want to engage with your teen?

- What parenting principle or idea do you want to remember from this chapter?

Reflection Questions
Principles for Parents: Thinking Biblically

I love yummy food. I can talk on and on about the little hole-in-the-wall restaurant with the most amazing chicken gravy (and how it's perfect for dipping with their hush puppies). Or where to get the best salted caramel brownie in town. Or the freshest acai bowl. And don't get me started talking about my favorite pizza places. That might take hours of your time!

When we're excited about something, we want to talk about it. And naturally, we share our excitement with others in a compelling way.

When it comes to sharing God's Word with our teens, one of the most important aspects is that we enjoy it ourselves. As we meditate and reflect upon God's Word, it naturally overflows into our interactions with our teens. Read Deuteronomy 6:1-9, and answer the following questions.

1. In this passage, Moses is speaking to the people of Israel. What does he tell them to do?

2. Consider verses 1-3. Why does Moses want them to obey God's commands? In what ways is it a blessing to them?

3. Consider verses 4-6. What is asked of parents in this passage?

4. How would you describe your affection for the Lord today? Is it warm, lukewarm, or perhaps cold?

5. How is your time in the Word? Do you enjoy reading the Bible? Is it difficult for you? Why or why not?

6. What is one way you could be listening to God's Word more this week? Perhaps you set aside some time to read it each day, or listen to a Bible app on your way to work, or memorize a Bible verse. What would help you reflect upon God more as you go through your day? If your desire for God is cold, begin each day by praying, "Refresh my heart, O God. Give me a deeper desire to know you."

7. Consider verses 7-9. How does this passage instruct us to engage with our children?

8. Do you feel comfortable talking with your teen about the Bible? Why or why not?

9. What's a practical way you could talk with your teen this week about God or the Bible?

In addition to enjoying food, I also love to garden. Every spring, I watch with amazement as tomatoes slowly grow on the vine. I spend the summer enjoying the produce. By the end of fall, the first freeze comes, and it's time to clear out the old vines.

Clearing the garden is easy work because once vines are dead, they lose all their strength and break apart with little effort. A detached vine crumbles to dust with the slightest touch. Perhaps that's why Jesus chose to use the image of a vine when he commanded us to abide in him, warning that apart from him, we can do nothing.

10. Read John 15:4-11.

    a. From what you read in this passage, what does it mean to abide in Jesus? Why is this so important?

    b. What type of fruit do you think Jesus is talking about here? (See Galatians 5:22.) What impact would bearing that type of fruit have on your parenting?

    c. List some of the results of abiding. Which one of these results are you longing for today?

Purposeful Parenting: Engaging Gracefully

The survey findings presented in *Handing Down the Faith* led to these observations:

The most effective parent conversations about religion with children are children-centered rather than parent-centered. In them, children ask questions and talk more while parents mostly listen; the questions about religion are clearly related to the children's lives; parents try to help children understand their religious faith and practices; the conversations are open, not rigid or highly controlled; and the larger relationship between parents and children is thereby nurtured. When parents, by contrast, talk too much, make demands without explanations, force unwanted conversations, and restrict discussions to topics that they control, faith transmission to children is likely to be ineffective or counterproductive.[1]

11. How would you describe your conversations with your teen about God, faith, and the Bible? Are these comfortable or uncomfortable conversations in your home? Why or why not?

12. When your teen has questions about the Bible, how do you respond? How could you make your conversations more open and less rigid?

13. In what ways could you invite your teen to ask more questions about the Bible? How could you be a better listener?

Practical Advice: Living Wisely

14. How would you describe the home in which you grew up: negligent/absentee, permissive/indulgent, authoritative/shepherding, authoritarian/domineering?

15. How would you describe your parenting style? Do you lean more toward permissive or authoritarian? How would you describe your spouse's parenting style?

16. In what ways can you be more shepherdlike in your parenting this week? How can you lead with expectations, patience, gentleness, warmth, and responsiveness?

Request

1. As you think about your teen(s) today, what is your specific prayer for them?

2. As you think about your parenting, in what ways do you need the Lord's help?

Spend some time in prayer, using these verses to guide you:

> Teach me, O LORD, the way of your statutes;
>   and I will keep it to the end.
> Give me understanding, that I may keep your law
>   and observe it with my whole heart.
> Lead me in the path of your commandments,
>   for I delight in it.
> Incline my heart to your testimonies,
>   and not to selfish gain!
> Turn my eyes from looking at worthless things;
>   and give me life in your ways.
>
> —Psalm 119:33-37

Group Discussion Questions

If you are going through the *Parenting with Hope* book and study guide with your spouse or a group, be sure to continue with the group discussion questions for Lesson 1, beginning on page 99.

LESSON 2

The Power of His Presence: Prayer

Give ear, O LORD, to my prayer; listen to
my plea for grace (Psalm 86:6).

Read

In your copy of *Parenting with Hope*, read chapter 2, "The Power of His Presence: Prayer," and then take a moment to write down your responses to the questions below.

Respond

- What biblical principles stood out to you in this chapter?

- In what ways did this chapter impact how you want to engage with your teen?

- What parenting principle or idea do you want to remember from this chapter?

Reflection Questions
Principles for Parents: Thinking Biblically

When Mike and I first got married, we moved more than 2,000 miles from Raleigh, North Carolina, to Mesa, Arizona. I remember buying a paper map, studying it intently, and writing out directions as I tried to navigate a new city. These days, traveling in a new city is much easier. I simply type an address into my smartphone, and Google maps guides me for every twist and turn. I can even choose a lovely British accent to guide me on my way.

When it comes to parenting teens, most of us would welcome some directional support. We'd even be happy with a paper map. While we don't have specific instructions, thankfully, God guides us by his Word and gives us wisdom and guidance through prayer. Everyone's specific circumstances are different, but God offers wisdom for anyone who calls on his name. As we think about the power of prayer, begin by reading Matthew 6:7-13.

1. Why is it significant that we pray to "Our Father in heaven"?

2. What is the first request in this prayer? What does that request mean?

3. What does it mean to pray "Your will be done"? In what ways does this reorient our desires about our teens?

4. In what circumstance or situation with your teen right now do you need God's daily sustaining power?

5. As you think about your interactions with your teen this past week, is there anything for which you need to ask their forgiveness?

6. As you think about your teen, in what ways are they struggling with temptation? Take a moment to pray for them in their struggle, that the Lord would deliver them from all evil.

7. Read Colossians 1:9-12, Philippians 1:9-11, and 2 Thessalonians 1:9-12. These are examples of some of the ways Paul prayed for his spiritual children in the faith.

   a. What types of requests does Paul make in these verses?

   b. How are these requests similar to or different from your own prayers?

   c. What do you learn from Paul's prayers that you can apply to your own life?

Purposeful Parenting: Engaging Gracefully

Take a moment to read the following verses, and consider the various ways we are taught to pray for one another:

- "Rejoice in hope, be patient in tribulation, be constant in prayer" (Romans 12:12).

- "I urge that supplications, prayers, intercessions, and thanksgivings be made for all people, for kings and all who are in high positions, that we may lead a peaceful and quiet life, godly and dignified in every way" (1 Timothy 2:1-2).

- "Continue steadfastly in prayer, being watchful in it with thanksgiving. At the same time, pray also for us, that God may open to us a door for the word, to declare the mystery of Christ" (Colossians 4:2-3).

- "The harvest is plentiful, but the laborers are few. Therefore, pray earnestly to the Lord of the harvest to send out laborers into his harvest" (Luke 10:2).

- "Is anyone among you suffering? Let him pray. Is anyone cheerful? Let him sing praise. Is anyone among you sick? Let him call for the elders of the church, and let them pray over him, anointing him with oil in the name of the Lord" (James 5:13-14).

8. This week, I encourage you to think of some ways you can pray together as a family. Take a few moments now to list some specific people you can pray for:

   a. Members of your family

  b. Leaders in your community (bosses, presidents, principals, pastors)

  c. Missionaries from your church or whom you support

  d. Neighbors and world events

9. What would it look like for your family to pray together for these needs? When could you set aside time to pray together?

10. What is your teen feeling anxious or concerned about? How could you encourage them through prayer?

Practical Advice: Living Wisely

11. In what ways do prayer and God's Word work together as you create rules in your home?

12. As you enter into parenting during the teen years, are there any family rules that you need to readjust or reconsider?

13. In what areas are you particularly anxious about your child today? In the space provided, list the specific concerns you have.

Request

1. As you think about your teen(s) today, what is your specific prayer for them?

2. As you think about your parenting, in what ways do you
    need the Lord's help?

Spend some time in prayer, using this passage to guide you:

> It is my prayer that your love may abound more
> and more, with knowledge and all discernment,
> so that you may approve what is excellent, and so
> be pure and blameless for the day of Christ, filled
> with the fruit of righteousness that comes through
> Jesus Christ, to the glory and praise of God.
>
> —Philippians 1:9-11

Group Discussion Questions

If you are going through the *Parenting with Hope* book and
study guide with your spouse or a group, be sure to continue with
the group discussion questions for Lesson 2, beginning on page
105.

Our Home Away from Home: The Church

Christ is the head of the church, his body, and is himself its Savior (Ephesians 5:23).

Read

In your copy of *Parenting with Hope*, read chapter 3, "Our Home Away from Home: The Church," and then take a moment to write down your responses to the questions below.

Respond

- What biblical principles stood out to you in this chapter?

- In what ways did this chapter impact how you want to engage with your teen?

- What parenting principle or idea do you want to remember from this chapter?

Reflection Questions
Principles for Parents: Thinking Biblically

In 2020, the world changed seemingly overnight. As COVID-19 spread across the globe, stores and restaurants were closed, flights were grounded, and most churches stopped having in-person gatherings. We all felt the painful effects of isolation. It became abundantly clear: technology can only do so much to connect us. It's not good to be alone. It matters that we're physically together because we need one another.

Our teens are looking for community. They are desperate to belong, and the church provides a healthy home for their longings. Read Hebrews 10:22-25.

1. This passage has three communal commands that begin with the phrase, "Let us…" List the three actions we are to do together as a church.

2. Why are each of these three actions so important? How have you experienced encouragement like this through the church?

3. Read Ephesians 4:11-16. Why do you think meeting together as a church is so important for spiritual health?

4. Read 1 Corinthians 12:18-27.

   a. Why might we be tempted to think we don't need each other in the church? In what ways is it easier than ever to be distanced from being a part of a local congregation?

   b. How does this passage explain both our individuality and our sense of belonging?

c. From what you read in this chapter, why do you think church is so important for teens, especially in an age of increased cell phone use and isolation?

5. How has the church helped you to grow in the faith? What benefits have you experienced from being a member of a church?

6. In what ways have you seen the church be a blessing for your children?

Purposeful Parenting: Engaging Gracefully

According to a study from Harvard T.H. Chan School of Public Health:

> Researchers found that people who attended weekly religious services or practiced daily prayer or meditation in their youth reported greater life satisfaction and positivity in their 20s—and were less likely to subsequently have depressive symptoms, smoke, use illicit drugs, or have a sexually transmitted infection—than people raised with less regular spiritual habits.[2]

7. Read Proverbs 18:1.

   a. What does this proverb warn against?

   b. In what ways have you seen this principle at work in your own life or the lives of others?

   c. In what ways can you encourage your teen toward healthy community?

8. How does your teen feel about going to church? In what ways are they participating in the life of the church?

9. How involved is your family in the life of the church? In what areas are you currently serving and using your gifts? In what ways would you like to be more involved?

10. Where is your teen using their gifts in the church? How could you help them find ways to actively serve others?

11. What are some of the reasons it can be difficult to get to church on a weekly basis? Why would you say it is worth it for your family?

Practical Advice: Living Wisely

12. How would you describe your church culture with regard to teens?

13. Does everyone in your church choose the same school options or have similar family rules? Or do you see a range of parenting practices within your community? How well do you feel like you fit into the parenting styles of other parents in your church?

14. What would it look like for your family to practice Sabbath rest on Sunday? What are some ways your family could spend the Sabbath for the purpose of worshipping God and fellowshipping with his people?

Request

1. As you think about your teen(s) today, what is your specific prayer for them?

2. As you think about your parenting, in what ways do you need the Lord's help?

Spend some time in prayer, using these verses to guide you:

> Let us consider how to stir up one another to love and good works, not neglecting to meet together, as is the habit of some, but encouraging one another, and all the more as you see the Day drawing near.

—Hebrews 10:24-25

Group Discussion Questions

If you are going through the *Parenting with Hope* book and study guide with your spouse or a group, be sure to continue with the group discussion questions for Lesson 3, beginning on page 111.

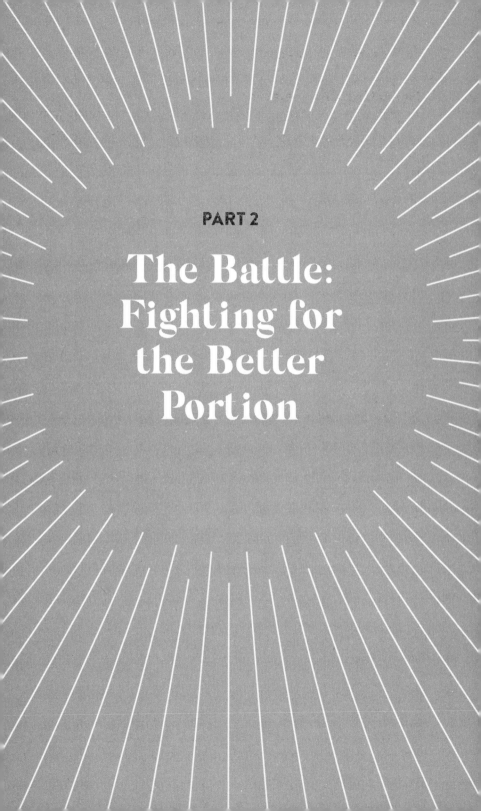

PART 2

The Battle: Fighting for the Better Portion

Questions to Consider

Even while these people were worshiping the LORD, they were
serving their idols. To this day their children and grandchildren
continue to do as their ancestors did (2 Kings 17:41 NIV).

I encourage you to use these questions to help guide you as you begin Section 2. The questions in this section are for personal reflection. There won't be group discussion questions for this introduction to Section 2 because this isn't a full chapter.

Read

In your copy of *Parenting with Hope*, read the introduction to Section 2: "The Battle: Fighting for the Better Portion." Then take a moment to write down your responses to the questions below.

Respond

* What biblical principles stood out to you in this section?

- In what ways did this section impact how you want to engage with your teen?

- What parenting principle or idea do you want to remember from this section?

Reflection Questions

Source idols are the motivating factors underneath the idols that rise to the surface. Each of these four source idols has different motivations, emotions, and fears. Within the following descriptions, underline which source idols you tend to struggle with the most (and it's possible you may underline more than one):

The source idol of *power* is usually at the core of a person who is driven by success, influence, recognition, or supremacy. They will usually be competitive and confident, while struggling with emotions of anger and frustration. They are willing to be overburdened with responsibility, and their core fear is humiliation.[3]

The source idol of *approval* is usually at the core of a person who is driven by a desire for love, affirmation, acceptance, and connection. They will usually be likeable while struggling with emotions of fear and cowardice. Their core fear is rejection, and they may be overly sensitive or insecure in relationships.

The source idol of *comfort* is usually at the core of a person who is driven by a desire for ease, pleasure, and a lack of stress. They will usually be easygoing and less productive while struggling with feelings of boredom. Their core fears are stress and demands, which can lead to others feeling hurt or neglected.

The source idol of *control* is usually at the core of a person who is driven by rules, routines, and everything going according to their plan. They will usually be competent and individualistic, while struggling with feelings of anxiety. They may experience loneliness, and their core fears are uncertainty, unpredictable circumstances, and unreliable people.

In addition to source idols, we have plenty of other idols springing up to the surface. *Surface idols* can include appearance, work, money, family, friendships, school choices, social status, materialism, health, ideology, ministry, and a variety of other items that we rely on for our significance and value. It may take some thoughtful time of reflection to spot surface idols in our lives. Take a few moments to reflect upon the following questions to help you identify various surface idols in your life:

1. Who/what do you fear losing? Who/what do you love?

2. What do you spend your time on?

3. What do you spend money on?

4. What do you think about on a regular basis?

5. What do you trust in for security or comfort? What do you hope in?

6. What do you want that others have?

7. What do you respect in others?

As you consider these questions, think about how your answers impact your hopes and dreams for your teen. List a few ways your source idols may be springing to the surface in your parenting:

Request

Spend some time in prayer, using these verses to guide you:

> I will sprinkle clean water on you, and you shall

be clean from all your uncleannesses, and from all
your idols I will cleanse you. And I will give you a
new heart, and a new spirit I will put within you.
And I will remove the heart of stone from your
flesh and give you a heart of flesh. And I will put
my Spirit within you, and cause you to walk in
my statutes and be careful to obey my rules.

—Ezekiel 36:25-28

The Secret of True Success: (Isn't) Scholarship and Affluence

The fear of the LORD is the beginning of wisdom, and the knowledge of the Holy One is insight (Proverbs 9:10).

Read

In your copy of *Parenting with Hope*, read chapter 4, "The Secret of True Success: (Isn't) Scholarship and Affluence," and then take a moment to write down your responses to the questions below.

Respond

- What biblical principles stood out to you in this chapter?

- In what ways did this chapter impact how you want to engage with your teen?

- What parenting principle or idea do you want to remember from this chapter?

Reflection Questions

Principles for Parents: Thinking Biblically

When asked what they want for their children, many parents reply, "I just want them to be happy." However, the way we envision their happiness tells a lot about what's happening in our hearts. As you think about the future, what do you want most for them? Are you hoping for a good college and well-paying job? It's easy to trust in money because, on the surface, it appears to offer so much.

Hebrews warns and instructs us, "Keep your life free from love of money, and be content with what you have, for he has said, 'I will never leave you nor forsake you'" (13:5). We need to put off a love of money and put on contentment. How can we do this? By remembering that the Lord is with us. Money is fleeting. Success is temporary. The Lord's presence is eternal. Today, we'll consider some proverbs to glean wisdom to guide us as we parent our teens.

1. Read Psalm 112:1-3, Proverbs 12:27, Proverbs 13:22, and Proverbs 14:24. What principles about wealth do you learn from these passages?

2. Read Proverbs 22:16, Proverbs 28:8, Ecclesiastes 5:10, and 1 Timothy 6:10. What do we learn about the love of money? How do you see these principles in society today?

3. As you read these verses, how would you describe your view of money? Are you a spender or a saver? How does having money affect your feelings of security, happiness, or generosity? How does a lack of money cause you to fear, worry, or be anxious?

4. When you think about the source idols you struggle with most (power, approval, control, or comfort), how do they rise to the surface with your teens regarding money and schoolwork?

5. Read Colossians 3:23-24. How can we have right expectations about our teen's schoolwork? What would it look like to focus on their work ethic over their grades?

6. What hopes and dreams are you regularly communicating to your teen? What's the emphasis of your home? Are your words and example demonstrating biblical truth or worldly wisdom?

Purposeful Parenting: Engaging Gracefully

Madeline Levine wisely explains, "The creativity and flexibility required to become a true learner is inhibited by excessive focus on every inch of progress, or lack thereof. It may keep a kid's nose to the grindstone because she is anxious about her performance, but it certainly does not encourage a real love of learning."[4]

7. What is the difference between valuing learning over grades? What would you say your family values more?

8. In what ways do you fall into the misguided belief pattern that academic success = material success = happiness? How does that affect your parenting?

9. What would it look like in the home to value character first, effort second, and grades last? If you asked your teen, what do you think they would say you value most?

10. There's a big difference between helping your teen with homework and doing the work for them. In what ways do you need to let your child do their work more independently?

11. How much tension do you experience in your home because of schoolwork and grades? What would you like to change about how you engage with your teen in this area?

Practical Advice: Living Wisely

12. Even though they look more and more like adults, our teens' brains aren't fully formed. How can that knowledge prompt you to be more compassionate in your responses to their forgetfulness?

13. In what ways can you help create healthy rhythms in your home to encourage positive learning environments?

14. How difficult is it for you to let your child take responsibility for their homework? Why is it important that they learn to manage it on their own during the teen years?

15. In what ways can you communicate to your teen that they are valued for who they are (made in the image of God) rather than how they perform academically?

Request

1. As you think about your teen(s) today, what is your specific prayer for them?

2. As you think about your parenting, in what ways do you need the Lord's help?

Spend some time in prayer, using this verse to guide you:

A good name is to be chosen rather than great riches, and favor is better than silver or gold.

—Proverbs 22:1

Group Discussion Questions

If you are going through the *Parenting with Hope* book and study guide with your spouse or a group, be sure to continue with the group discussion questions for Lesson 4, beginning on page 117.

Beware of Busyness: Sports and Activities

Rather train yourself for godliness; for while bodily training is of some value, godliness is of value in every way, as it holds promise for the present life and also for the life to come (1 Timothy 4:7-8).

Read

In your copy of *Parenting with Hope*, read chapter 5, "Beware of Busyness: Sports and Activities," and then take a moment to write down your responses to the questions below.

Respond

- What biblical principles stood out to you in this chapter?

- In what ways did this chapter impact how you want to engage with your teen?

- What parenting principle or idea do you want to remember from this chapter?

Reflection Questions
Principles for Parents: Thinking Biblically

Honestly, I have no interest in professional sports. I'm shocked at what people pay to attend games. They just aren't that exciting to me. However, the thought of watching my daughter play soccer for her high school? I'm there with bells on—so go ahead and pass the stale popcorn.

Throughout the years, my husband and I have loved sitting on the sidelines watching our kids play soccer, baseball, track, volleyball, and church league basketball. We've enjoyed school musicals, plays, and squeaky violin concerts. We've watched rocket launches and attended art shows.

It's a joy to watch our kids participate in all sorts of activities. However, it's also good for us to give careful thought to our schedules. We want our time spent on activities to rightly represent what we value.

1. Read 1 Timothy 4:7-8 and Hebrews 12:11.

a. What are the benefits and value of sports and activities for our kids?

b. What are the limitations?

2. How have you seen physical or musical training teach you spiritual truths? What benefits have you experienced? What benefits have you seen for your teen?

3. Read Romans 12:9-11. How can we encourage our teens with these verses as they engage in competitive activities?

4. What activities were you involved in during your teen years? How does that affect your hopes and dreams for your teen?

5. Is there time in your teen's schedule for personal Bible reading, prayer, and church events?

Purposeful Parenting: Engaging Gracefully

6. How can sports and activities become an idol in parents' lives? How have you seen this played out in your community?

7. Consider your source idols (power, approval, comfort, control). How do they come to the surface with regard to your teen's activities?

8. On a scale of 1 to 10 (with 10 being the busiest), how would you rank your home? Are you comfortable with that number?

9. Do your kids ever have time to be bored? What have you seen them create or do when they have less busy schedules?

10. How much sleep does your teen get each night? How is that affecting them?

Practical Advice: Living Wisely

As we think about busy schedules and how they impact family meals, Madeline Levine says:

> Perhaps the single most important ritual a family can observe is having dinner together. Families who eat together five or more times a week have kids who are significantly less likely to use tobacco, alcohol, or marijuana, have higher grade-point averages, less depressive symptoms, and fewer suicide attempts than families who eat together two or fewer times a week.[5]

11. How often do you have family meals together? How would you like that number to change?

12. What do you do when sports or other activities interfere with church? How can we value what is most important for their spiritual development over their physical development?

13. Think through a particular activity your teen is interested in and consider:

    a. Why does my teen want to do this activity?

    b. Will this activity prevent healthy sleep habits?

    c. Will this activity keep us out of church regularly?

    d. Will this activity interfere with family dinners?

e. Will this activity prevent free time?

Request

1. As you think about your teen(s) today, what is your specific prayer for them?

2. As you think about your parenting, in what ways do you need the Lord's help?

Spend some time in prayer, using this verse to guide you:

So teach us to number our days that
we may get a heart of wisdom.

—Psalm 90:12

Group Discussion Questions

If you are going through the *Parenting with Hope* book and study guide with your spouse or a group, be sure to continue with the group discussion questions for Lesson 5, beginning on page 121.

The Pitfalls of Popularity: Social Acceptance

Our citizenship is in heaven, and from it we await a Savior,
the Lord Jesus Christ, who will transform our lowly body
to be like his glorious body, by the power that enables him
even to subject all things to himself (Philippians 3:20).

Read

In your copy of *Parenting with Hope*, read chapter 6, "The Pitfalls of Popularity: Social Acceptance," and then take a moment to write down your responses to the questions below.

Respond

- What biblical principles stood out to you in this chapter?

- In what ways did this chapter impact how you want to engage with your teen?

- What parenting principle or idea do you want to remember from this chapter?

Reflection Questions
Principles for Parents: Thinking Biblically

Most of us have had those moments of insecurity when we wonder, *Where do I fit in? Will other people accept me? Who are my friends?* As we watch our children head into new environments in middle school and high school, some of our own fears about social acceptance rise to the surface.

As parents, it's tough to navigate new experiences with our teens. We want to offer perspective as well as sympathy. We want to help them develop good friendships (which they need), yet avoid being overinvolved in relationship dramas. Our teens need our help socially, but they want independence. It's helpful to think deeply about what it means to set our hearts on pilgrimage as we parent our teens.

1. Read Philippians 1:9-11. Why do we have to have different affections if we want to parent our children with different hopes?

2. Read Philippians 3:17-21. What does it mean to be a citizen of heaven? How should that affect our parenting?

3. How is your parenting different than the parenting of others because of your faith?

4. Read 1 Peter 2:11-12. Why do Christians have different rules than other people? What effect does this have on those who do not believe?

5. How do the rules of your home seek to obey God and bless others?

Purposeful Parenting: Engaging Gracefully

6. When your teen looks at your life, do they see you living differently from the world around you? How do they see you using your time, talents, and treasure? What types of friends do they see you prioritizing? How would they evaluate your screen time or your social interactions with others?

7. How can we engage with our teens when they feel different from others because of their faith?

8. When your teen experiences loneliness or is excluded, how do you help them have perspective? What would be a wrong response in that situation?

9. If your child is in the popular group, are they aware of other teens' feelings? Do they seek to include others? Are they kind and loving to those who may not fit in as well? Are they choosing healthy friendships that encourage their faith?

10. How does your desire for acceptance affect your parenting? How do you think your anxiety about your teen's social acceptance affects them?

11. When have you led with a rule when it would have been wiser to lead with a conversation?

12. Would your teen consider you a good listener? Why or why not? In what ways could you improve?

Practical Advice: Living Wisely

While social media claims to offer connection and community, the results are actually the opposite: "Those who visit social media sites every day or nearly every day are 11% more likely to be lonely. It's non-screen activities that help teens feel less alone, not social media. The loneliest teens are those who spend more time on social media and less time with their friends in person."[6]

13. Are you surprised by the data on smartphones? What stood out to you?

14. What do you think are some healthy guidelines for social media and smartphones?

15. What ways can you educate your teen about sex, smartphones, or alcohol use without lecturing them? Why are these conversations so important?

Request

1. As you think about your teen(s) today, what is your specific prayer for them?

2. As you think about your parenting, in what ways do you need the Lord's help?

Spend some time in prayer, using this verse to guide you:

Whoever walks with the wise becomes wise, but
the companion of fools will suffer harm.

—Proverbs 13:20

Group Discussion Questions

If you are going through the *Parenting with Hope* book and study guide with your spouse or a group, be sure to continue with the group discussion questions for Lesson 6, beginning on page 125.

PART 3

The Blessings: Cultivating a Home Where Teens Thrive

Acceptance: A Home of Grace

By grace you have been saved through faith. And this is not your own doing; it is the gift of God, not a result of works, so that no one may boast (Ephesians 2:8-9).

Read

In your copy of *Parenting with Hope*, read chapter 7, "Acceptance: A Home of Grace," and then take a moment to write down your responses to the questions below.

Respond

- What biblical principles stood out to you in this chapter?

- In what ways did this chapter impact how you want to engage with your teen?

- What parenting principle or idea do you want to remember from this chapter?

Reflection Questions
Principles for Parents: Thinking Biblically

We've all made our fair share of mistakes. Our teens will make them too. One important lesson we sometimes forget to teach is: *How do I deal with failure?* We want our teens to know what to do when they sin against others, as well as know how to respond to someone else's sin.

As we live side by side with our teens, some of the most important lessons are happening through our daily responses to our children's failures and successes. These seemingly insignificant interactions profoundly impact our teens. We want to create a home where apologies are offered regularly and forgiveness is freely given. What we teach through our words will be significantly impressed upon our teens by our actions. We'll start today by studying the story of the unmerciful servant. Read Matthew 18:23-35.

1. What did the first servant owe the master? What about the second servant? What's the difference between those two amounts?

2. Why was the response of the servant to his fellow servant such a problem?

3. As parents, in what ways can we be like the unmerciful servant? Do we expect patience and forgiveness from God but fail to extend it to our teens?

4. In what ways can a lack of grace show up in your parenting? Think back to this past week. Are there any situations you wish you would have reacted differently to?

5. Read Luke 11:4 and Philippians 3:12. What do these passages tell us about our lives? How do these verses help give us realistic expectations of our teens?

6. Think about a time when you made a mistake as a teenager. What was your parents' response? What did they do right in their response? What did they do wrong?

Purposeful Parenting: Engaging Gracefully

It is a grace to our teens when we give them rules alongside warmth and relational engagement. They need both. In their research, Smith and Adamczyk explain:

> Combining clear and implemented life standards and expectations for their children with expressive emotional warmth and relational bonding with their children fosters relationships that most enhance effective religious transmission to children. Comparatively, independent of other religious factors that also matter, parents who are more permissive, disengaged, and authoritarian are simply less successful in passing on their religion to their offspring.[7]

7. Is grace in opposition to rules or consequences? Why or why not?

8. When your teen makes a mistake, how do you typically respond? How would you like to respond?

9. What is the difference between personal consequences and personal criticism?

10. Read Proverbs 12:18. Why are words so powerful? How have you seen their impact (for good or for bad) in your own life?

11. What is the problem with favoritism in the home? Do you favor one of your children over the others? Does your spouse?

12. As you think about specific situations involving your teen, what are some healthy consequences for your child?

Practical Advice: Living Wisely

A poor apology is one that blames someone else for your behavior: "I'm sorry you feel that way," or "I'm sorry for getting angry, but you made me mad because you did something wrong." A healthy apology accepts responsibility without lowering expectations: "I'm sorry I yelled at you for walking into the house with dirt all over your shoes. That was wrong, and I shouldn't have spoken harshly. Next time, can you please remember to take your shoes off before coming into the house?"

13. Consider your apologies. Do you give healthy apologies? In what ways could you accept responsibility when you apologize?

14. How can you "remember the relationship" in your parenting? Practically speaking, what would that look like in your home?

15. In what ways is it difficult for you to accept God's design, providence, and mission for your teen? How would you like to be more accepting in your parenting?

Request

1. As you think about your teen(s) today, what is your specific prayer for them?

2. As you think about your parenting, in what ways do you need the Lord's help?

Spend some time in prayer, using this verse to guide you:

Confess your sins to one another and pray for one another, that you may be healed. The prayer of a righteous person has great power as it is working.

—James 5:16

Group Discussion Questions

If you are going through the *Parenting with Hope* book and study guide with your spouse or a group, be sure to continue with the group discussion questions for Lesson 7, beginning on page 129.

Availability: A Home of Welcome

God is our refuge and strength, an ever-present help in trouble (Psalm 46:1).

Read

In your copy of *Parenting with Hope*, read chapter 8, "Availability: A Home of Welcome," and then take a moment to write down your responses to the questions below.

Respond

- What biblical principles stood out to you in this chapter?

- In what ways did this chapter impact how you want to engage with your teen?

• What parenting principle or idea do you want to remember from this chapter?

Reflection Questions
Principles for Parents: Thinking Biblically

When my children were young and had a bad dream, they called out to me in the night. As I sleepily walked into their room, I'd crawl into their bed and snuggle up next to them. I couldn't really do anything about their fears except offer my presence. Somehow, that was exactly what they needed.

Our teens may not call out to us in the same way, but they still need our presence. When they feel anxious or fearful, it helps them to know we are there for them. During these years, we may be tempted to think our presence is unwanted. However, I've found most teens welcome the involvement of their parents. Yes, they want their independence, but they still want to know we are there when they need us.

1. Read Joshua 1:6-9.

   a. What would Joshua have to be fearful of at this time?

b. What does God promise Joshua? What does he command of him?

c. How does God's promised presence with Joshua encourage you as you parent your teen today?

d. What are you fearful of as you parent today? What would it look like to call out to God in your fears and be comforted by his presence?

2. Read Romans 8:26-39.

a. What truths communicated in this passage encourage you today as the parent of a teen?

b. How do we see all the members of the Trinity (Father, Son, and Holy Spirit) actively present in this passage?

c. Think about some of the concerns and fears you have as you parent today. How does this passage give you hope in the midst of those fears?

3. Read Proverbs 18:1 and Proverbs 29:15. What do these two proverbs warn against? How do you think these principles apply to our teens?

4. Read Psalm 46. What truths about God are communicated in this psalm? What difference would it make in your parenting if you reminded yourself of these truths on a regular basis?

Purposeful Parenting: Engaging Gracefully

Our teens need the accountability of an adult's presence. Even though they may be able to be left alone, we need to be careful about too many hours left on their own. *The Price of Privilege* warns against this type of absentee parenting:

> Many parents at this stage feel that they've done their job and their children are old enough to manage on their own. Parents back off in all areas except academics, leaving their kids home alone after school or even

on occasional weekends. Kids this age need adult super-
vision because too much freedom leaves them vulnera-
ble to their own underdeveloped judgment. We know
that kids who start experimenting with drugs or alcohol
in early adolescence are at heightened risk for substance
abuse later. It is important for parents to work at main-
taining connection with their young teens in spite of
the protest, and even rejection, typical of this age. Eye
rolling passes, but the protection that parental involvement confers lasts a lifetime.[8]

5. Why does our presence as parents matter in our teens'
   lives? How can busyness or distractedness impact our
   parenting?

6. In what ways can you slow down and listen to your teen
   better?

7. How can being too quick to speak or offer advice come
   across to our teens as disinterest or condescension?

8. What is the difference between being available for our teens and being overinvolved in their lives? How would you describe yourself? In what ways can you improve?

9. Why are chores so important for teens? What chores do your teens do (or could they be doing) around the home?

Practical Advice: Living Wisely

10. Think about your current schedule. In what ways would saying no to more activities help you say yes to being available? What could you cut from your schedule? What would you like to add?

11. In what ways do you share about your life with your teen? How can you let your children get to know you in new ways as they enter the teen years?

12. What does it look like to be available to your teen, but also have necessary boundaries on your time?

13. Why does the statement "You're only as happy as your least happy child" put a lot of pressure on your teen? What (or who) should be the source of our contentment?

14. What are you currently doing for your teen that they could do for themselves? In what ways could you help them grow in independence?

Request

1. As you think about your teen(s) today, what is your specific prayer for them?

2. As you think about your parenting, in what ways do you need the Lord's help?

Spend some time in prayer, using these verses to guide you:

No, in all these things we are more than conquerors through him who loved us. For I am sure that neither death nor life, nor angels nor rulers, nor things present nor things to come, nor powers, nor height nor depth, nor anything else in all creation, will be able to separate us from the love of God in Christ Jesus our Lord.

—Romans 8:37-39

Group Discussion Questions

If you are going through the *Parenting with Hope* book and study guide with your spouse or a group, be sure to continue with the group discussion questions for Lesson 8, beginning on page 133.

Affection: A Home of Warmth

So now faith, hope, and love abide, these three; but the greatest of these is love (1 Corinthians 13:13).

Read

In your copy of *Parenting with Hope*, read chapter 9, "Affection: A Home of Warmth," and then take a moment to write down your responses to the questions below.

Respond

- What biblical principles stood out to you in this chapter?

- In what ways did this chapter impact how you want to engage with your teen?

- What parenting principle or idea do you want to remember from this chapter?

Reflection Questions
Principles for Parents: Thinking Biblically

Love. There's probably no other word that appears more in song titles. For example:

"All You Need Is Love"

"I Will Always Love You"

"Love Story"

"We Found Love"

"I Just Called to Say I Love You"

We sing happy songs about love. We sing sad songs, angry songs, and hopeful songs about it. We sing to memorialize old love and we sing in wonder of new love. Everyone wants to celebrate this "Crazy Little Thing Called Love."

More than anything, our teens need love from us. Love is the secret sauce that makes our homes full of joy and belonging. We should reflect the love God has for each of us, and this love prepares our children for loving others.

This will be our final chapter to study, and there's nothing more important we could discuss.

1. Read Mark 12:30-31. Why is it significant that the greatest two commandments are about love? How does what we love affect how we live?

2. Read 1 John 5:2-3. How do we know whether we love God? How do we know whether we love others?

3. In what ways does disobedience display a lack of love for God? How does our disobedience harm others, particularly those closest to us?

4. In what ways have you observed parents love their children more than God? What can you learn from the examples of Hannah and Eli? (see 1 Samuel 1–2). Why does the order of our affections matter?

5. Read 1 Corinthians 13:4-7. How do these verses encourage you to love your teen in new ways? What phrases in this passage do you find convicting?

6. Read 2 Timothy 3:1-17. What is hopeful about these words in the midst of a secular culture?

Purposeful Parenting: Engaging Gracefully

Loving our teen begins by loving God with all our heart, soul, mind, and strength. If we allow our affections to become misplaced or out of order, we'll find ourselves mired in fear, anxiety, and idolatry in our parenting. Instead, we want to parent with hope that flows from love. Our faithful example matters to our teen. *Handing Down the Faith* explains:

> Some readers might be surprised to know that the single, most powerful causal influence on the religious lives of American teenagers and young adults is the religious lives of their parents. Not their peers, not the media, not their youth group leaders or clergy, not their religious school teachers. Myriad studies show that, beyond a doubt, the parents of American youth play *the* leading role in shaping the character of their religious and spiritual lives, even well after they leave the home.[9]

7. In what ways have you seen your love for God impact your teen? If you asked your teen about your faith in God, how important would they say it is to you?

8. Loving our teens is not in opposition to correcting them. How can we lovingly correct rather than unkindly criticize? What's the difference?

9. What keeps you from "lighting up" when your teen walks into the room? How do you think your teen feels in your presence?

Practical Advice: Living Wisely

10. What makes a home warm and inviting? How can you create a sense of welcome for your family?

11. What does your family enjoy doing together for fun? How have you tried to create a warm environment in your home?

12. How do your teens receive love (words of affirmation, acts of service, physical touch, gifts, quality time)? Which of those is the most difficult for you to offer? Why?

13. In what ways can loving homes be outward focused, sharing the gospel with others? How can you invite others into your family to share the love of Christ?

Request

1. As you think about your teen(s) today, what is your specific prayer for them?

2. As you think about your parenting, in what ways do you need the Lord's help?

Spend some time in prayer, using these verses to guide you:

Love is patient and kind; love does not envy or boast;
it is not arrogant or rude. It does not insist on its

own way; it is not irritable or resentful; it does not
rejoice at wrongdoing, but rejoices with the truth.
Love bears all things, believes all things, hopes
all things, endures all things. Love never ends.

—1 Corinthians 13:4-8

Group Discussion Questions

If you are going through the *Parenting with Hope* book and
study guide with your spouse or a group, be sure to continue with
the group discussion questions for Lesson 9, beginning on page
137.

The Reason
We Can Parent
with Hope

As we come to the end of this study guide, I want to encourage you—the time you've spent studying the Bible and praying for your teens is some of the most important work you do as a parent. It matters. God's Word prepares your hearts and guides you in wisdom. Your prayers anchor you to God's power—he can work in ways beyond your comprehension. You don't have to solve all your parenting dilemmas. Keep looking to Jesus. He is your hope and guide as you parent your teen.

I also encourage you: keep having conversations with your teen. Ask good questions and offer biblical wisdom. Be kind and compassionate, patiently bearing with them when they make mistakes. Be slow to speak and quick to listen. Let them know every day, in every way, just how much you love them. Enjoy your teen—and light up when they walk in the room.

In our own strength, none of us feels up to this parenting task. None of us is able to be loving enough or kind enough or self-controlled enough. We all make mistakes. That's exactly why we keep going back to Jesus. He bears the fruit of the Spirit in us as we receive nourishment from him. We abide in his Word and his words abide in us. He forgives us, he changes us, and he proves time and again that his grace is sufficient. We're not powerless, because his power works mightily within us. All that we so desperately need as parents, Jesus freely gives.

So, I encourage you: keep walking with Jesus as you parent your teen. He's the sustainer of your faith and the substance of your hope. Rest in him and rely on him.

Jesus is the reason—the only reason—we can parent with hope.

PART 4

Group Discussion Questions

How to Use the Group Discussion Questions

I f you're meeting together as a group, the following questions are available to encourage and support your conversations. These questions are meant to be a general guide. Feel free to use only those that work best for your group or to add your own.

For each lesson, I've included an *icebreaker* and *opening question*, just to help start the discussion time. The icebreaker question is meant to be short and quick, allowing everyone an opportunity to answer. It's a fun way to help the group members get to know one another. Usually, the opening question is answered by only two or three people as a transition into the lesson. If time is short, or depending on your group dynamics, you may want to skip these questions.

As you discuss these topics with others, I encourage you to be thoughtful when you share about your teen. Be careful when you share about their sin struggles, hard days, or embarrassing moments, particularly in group settings. That doesn't mean you can't talk about your own struggles or concerns, but be considerate of your teen as you share. Commit to one another not to discuss what is shared during this time with others outside the group.

As you discuss these topics, support and encourage one another. Offer godly wisdom and advice, but avoid being overly prescriptive or judgmental toward others. We know only parts of one another's stories, and we are all carrying burdens that we can't always share in group settings. Prayerfully support one another when you are together, and continue to pray for one another through the week. I hope these times of discussion and prayer will richly bless you as you study God's Word together.

An Instruction Manual for Life: God's Word

GROUP DISCUSSION QUESTIONS

ICEBREAKER: If you could create a rule that everyone had to follow, what would it be?

OPENING QUESTION: What Bible passage has meant a lot to you in your life? Why?

1. Read Deuteronomy 6:1-9.

    a. What does this passage teach us about the importance of God's Word?

    b. In what ways are we to teach our children?

    c. Why is it so important that we love God's Word ourselves as we teach our children?

2. What are some of the reasons it's difficult to have a regular Bible reading habit? What has helped you to read the Bible on a regular basis?

3. How can we balance being rightly concerned about our children with not basing our contentment and peace on how they are doing? What would that look like in our parenting?

4. Read Psalm 1 and Jeremiah 17:7-8. In what ways does the image of a tree planted by streams of water help you as you consider the circumstances of your children today? How can you bear fruit in whatever you are facing today?

5. How has God's Word been a guide to you as a parent? A source of wisdom? Or refreshment? Or comfort?

6. What are some ways you try to engage your tweens or teens with God's Word? What has worked? What hasn't?

7. Read 2 Timothy 1:5 and 2 Timothy 3:15. What do these passages teach us about the importance of our example and God's Word as we parent our children?

8. Think back to conversations you've had with your teenagers this past week. What are some ways you could ask engaging questions rather than give answers? Why is this so difficult to do? Read the quote from *Handing Down the Faith* on page 16. How could you shape your conversations so they are more open and less rigid?

9. What type of home environment did you grow up in (permissive, authoritative, authoritarian, or uninvolved)? How would you describe your current parenting style?

10. In what ways can we teach our children with warmth and excitement rather than pressuring them? Why is it so important to have conversations with them rather than merely communicate our expectations?

Closing Prayer

Ask God to help you be a faithful example of loving him with all your heart, soul, mind, and strength. Also ask for opportunities to share God's Word with your teen this week.

The Power of His Presence: Prayer

GROUP DISCUSSION QUESTIONS

ICEBREAKER: What's your favorite way to get advice on a regular basis (Alexa, Google, books, etc.)?

OPENING QUESTION: Can you share about a time when God answered a specific prayer in a surprising or encouraging way?

1. Pastor Tim Keller defined prayer as a "personal, communicative response to the knowledge of God."[10] Why do you think people from all over the world pray regularly (even nonreligious people)?

2. Read Matthew 6:5-13.

    a. What does this passage teach you about how and when to pray?

    b. What does this passage teach you about what to pray for?

    c. How could the Lord's prayer help guide your prayers for your teen today?

3. What are some ways you've prayed with your children through the years? How do they respond to praying together as a family?

4. Why is prayer so important? How have you seen prayer work in your own life?

5. In what ways is prayer sometimes difficult?

6. What is the difference between scheduled prayer and spontaneous prayer? How would you like to grow in practicing these different types of prayer?

7. Read Philippians 1:9-11, Colossians 1:9-12, and 2 Thessalonians 1:9-12. These are examples of some of the ways Paul prayed for his spiritual children in the faith.

   a. What types of requests does Paul bring before the Lord in these verses?

   b. How are these requests similar to or different from your own prayers?

c. What do you learn from Paul's prayers that you can apply to your own life?

8. In what ways do prayer and God's Word work together as you create rules in your home?

9. What are the differences between permissive, authoritarian, and authoritative parenting? Do you struggle more in this season with being overly permissive or overly authoritarian?

10. In what areas are you particularly anxious about your child today? How could you trust God more in your parenting? What would that look like?

Closing Prayer

Ask God to help you be a praying parent. Also ask for opportunities to pray with your teen this week.

Our Home Away from Home: The Church

GROUP DISCUSSION QUESTIONS

ICEBREAKER: What's a group you've been a part of in which you felt like you really belonged? This could be something like a sports team, a work situation, a college group, or a neighborhood. What made you feel like a part of that group?

OPENING QUESTION: Can anyone share about a church they've been a part of that made them feel at home? What about that church made it welcoming?

1. Read Genesis 2:18-25.

   a. What problem do we encounter in this passage? What does God do to solve the problem? Why is it significant that this was a problem before sin entered the world?

   b. In what ways do you see the problem of loneliness in our world today? How has sin made the problem worse?

2. Read Hebrews 10:19-25.

   a. As you read this passage, what words are used to describe the communal nature of being a Christian?

   b. Why do you think it's so important for Christians to meet together regularly?

3. Read Proverbs 18:1.

a. What does this Proverb warn against?

b. In what ways have you seen this principle at work in your own life or the lives of others?

4. Read Acts 2:42-47.

a. Describe some of the aspects of the early church.

b. In what ways is this description similar to your church? In what ways are there differences?

5. Read 1 Corinthians 12:18-27.

a. Why might we be tempted to think we don't need each other in the church? In what ways is it easier than ever to be distanced from being a part of a local congregation?

b. How does this passage explain both our individuality and our sense of belonging?

c. From what you read in this chapter, why do you think church is so important for teens, especially in an age of increased cell phone use and isolation?

6. How would you describe your church culture with regard to teens? Does everyone in your church choose the same school options or have similar family rules? Or do you see a range of parenting practices within your community? How well do you feel like you fit into the parenting styles of those in your church?

7. What are some of the reasons it can be difficult to get to church on a weekly basis? Why would you say attending church is worthwhile for your family?

8. What would it look like for your family to practice Sabbath rest on Sunday? What are some ideas of ways you could spend the Sabbath for the purpose of worshipping God and fellowshipping with his people?

9. Read Romans 12:3-13.

   a. In what ways does this passage point to our need of one another?

   b. Why is humility a necessary part of being in community with others?

    c. Why is serving in the church so important? How is it part of loving others?

    d. In what ways can teens serve in their church communities? How can serving others be a blessing for them?

10. What are some of the blessings of being a part of a church community? How have you seen it impact your own life? How has it impacted your children?

Closing Prayer

Pray together for your churches, asking that they may be places of belonging and community for teens. Pray especially for teens in your congregations who may feel lonely or isolated.

The Secret of True Success: (Isn't) Scholarship and Affluence

GROUP DISCUSSION QUESTIONS

ICEBREAKER: If you could go to college today, what subject would you choose to study?

OPENING QUESTION: How (and why) do you think most people would answer this question: Would you rather be smart or rich?

1. Read Psalm 112:1-3, Proverbs 12:27, Proverbs 13:22, and Proverbs 14:24. What principles about wealth do you learn from these passages?

2. Read Proverbs 22:16, Proverbs 28:8, Ecclesiastes 5:10, and 1 Timothy 6:10. What do you learn about the love of money? How do you see these principles or observations on display in society today?

3. Money can't buy contentment. How do you see this reality in your own life and the lives of others? What can Hebrews 13:5 teach us about contentment? How can we impress that truth on our children?

4. Why do you think our society is so focused on academic success for our children today? In what ways is it tempting to value grades over an education? What type of learning environment does that create? How can this harm our teens?

5. In what ways do different source idols (power, control, comfort, approval) cause us to put pressure on our teens academically?

6. What would it look like in the home to value character first, effort second, and grades last? If you asked your teen, what do you think they would say you value most?

7. What would it look like to be gracious with your teen when they make mistakes in school? Can anyone share about a time when they failed to be gracious? What would you have done differently?

8. Why is it so important that our kids experience the natural consequences of their lack of hard work? Why is it wrong for us to do their work for them?

9. Why is it easy to fall into the misguided belief pattern that academic success = material success = happiness?

10. How can we raise hardworking teens who also know we value their character over their performance? What would that look like in the home?

Closing Prayer

Pray the protection of Proverbs 30:8 over your children's lives (and yours as well): "Remove far from me falsehood and lying; give me neither poverty nor riches; feed me with the food that is needful for me." Above all else, ask the Lord to give your children a deep contentment in God's presence in their lives and to guard them from the pitfalls of a love of money.

Beware of Busyness: Sports and Activities

GROUP DISCUSSION QUESTIONS

ICEBREAKER: What's your favorite sport?

OPENING QUESTION: Why do you think cultures all around the world find ways to engage in competition? What are some universal traits people enjoy about sports?

1. Read Hebrews 12:11. How does the discipline of playing a sport or instrument help teach us spiritual truths?

2. How can sports and activities become an idol in parents' lives? How have you seen this played out in your community?

3. What are some of the dangers for our kids when they are doing too much?

4. How can we teach our teens that we value character over competition?

5. Read Romans 12:9-11. How can we encourage our teens with these verses as they engage in competitive activities?

6. What are some signs of parental idolatry when it comes to sports and activities? How can we spot and be aware of our own struggles as parents?

7. Do your kids ever have time to be bored? What have you seen them create or do when they have less-busy schedules?

8. What should we do when sports or other activities interfere with church? How can we value what is most important for their spiritual development over their physical development?

9. Why do you think family dinners are so important for the healthy development of teens?

10. Read Colossians 3:23-24. How can this verse guide us as we make decisions about teens and their schedules?

Closing Prayer

Close your time together by asking God for wisdom for each family in your group as they make decisions about sports and activities. Encourage one another with James 1:5: "If any of you lacks wisdom, let him ask God, who gives generously to all without reproach, and it will be given him."

The Pitfalls of Popularity: Social Acceptance

ICEBREAKER: What was popular when you were in high school? (Consider clothing, hairstyles, or activities.)

OPENING QUESTION: What makes someone popular? What are some characteristics or qualities popular people often have?

1. Read Philippians 1:9-11. Why do we have to have different affections if we want to parent our children with different hopes?

2. Read Philippians 3:17-21. What does it mean to be a citizen of heaven? How should that affect our parenting?

3. How can we engage with our teens when they feel different or ostracized from others because of their faith?

4. Read 1 Peter 2:11-12. Why do Christians have different rules than other people? What effect does this have on those who do not believe?

5. When our children experience loneliness or are excluded, what can we do to help them have a healthy perspective? What would be a wrong response in that situation? How can we help our children to view, through a biblical lens, the lonely or outcast in their school? What should be our goal as parents as our teens build friendships with other teens?

6. How does our personal desire for acceptance affect our parenting? How do you think it affects teens when they sense our anxiety about their social acceptance?

7. How can we teach our children to "flee sexual immorality" (1 Corinthians 6:18) and pursue purity? Why is this important? Why is this difficult to do with so much access to smartphones and computers?

8. What do you think are some healthy guidelines for using social media and smartphones?

9. What is the difference between leading with a rule and leading with a conversation?

10. How can we give our teens facts to educate them about sex, smartphones, or alcohol use without lecturing them? What are some creative ways we can help them learn while engaging them in the process?

Closing Prayer

Pray together as a group, asking God to provide good friends for your teens. Let Proverbs 13:20 guide you: "Whoever walks with the wise becomes wise, but the companion of fools will suffer harm."

Acceptance: A Home of Grace

GROUP DISCUSSION QUESTIONS

ICEBREAKER: If you were caught stealing a cookie from a cookie jar, what type of cookie would you be stealing?

OPENING QUESTION: Can you share about a time in your life when you did something wrong and someone extended grace to you? How did that impact you?

1. Read Luke 11:4 and Philippians 3:12. What do these passages tell us about our lives? How do these verses help give us realistic expectations of our teens?

2. In what ways do you blame your impatience, anger, or harsh words on your teen's behavior? Why is that problematic?

3. Have you ever apologized to your teen? In what ways is doing this difficult? Why is it important to do?

4. Is grace in opposition to rules or consequences? Why or why not?

5. What is the difference between personal consequences and personal criticism?

6. Read Proverbs 12:18. Why are words so powerful? How have you seen their impact (for good or for bad) on your own life?

7. How can our words have unhealthy consequences on our teens? What are some examples of emotional manipulation, and why is such behavior harmful?

8. What are some healthy consequences to offer during the teen years?

9. Do you struggle with favoritism in your parenting? Why or why not? What are the likely negative effects of favoritism in the home?

10. How can you "remember the relationship" in your parenting? What would that look like practically in your home?

11. In what ways is it difficult for you to accept God's design, providence, and mission for your teen? How would you like to do that more in your parenting?

Closing Prayer

Close your time in prayer for one another, using James 5:16 to guide you: "Confess your sins to one another and pray for one another, that you may be healed. The prayer of a righteous person has great power as it is working."

Availability: A Home of Welcome

GROUP DISCUSSION QUESTIONS

ICEBREAKER: If you were playing a trivia game like "Who Wants to Be a Millionaire?," who would be your "phone a friend" lifeline?

OPENING QUESTION: Can you share about a time when someone's presence in your life really mattered to you?

1. Read Romans 8:26-39.

   a. What truths communicated in this passage encourage you today as the parent of a teen?

b. How do we see all the members of the Trinity (Father, Son, and Holy Spirit) actively present in this passage?

c. Think about some of the concerns and fears you have in parenting today. How does this passage give you hope in the midst of those fears?

2. Read Proverbs 18:1 and Proverbs 29:15. What do these two proverbs warn against? How do you think these principles apply to our teens?

3. Read Psalm 46. What truths about God are communicated in this psalm? What difference would it make in your parenting if you reminded yourself of these truths on a regular basis?

4. Why does our presence as parents matter in our teens' lives? How can busyness or distractedness impact our parenting?

5. Why is listening an important part of our availability? How can being too quick to speak or offer advice come across to our teens as disinterest or condescension?

6. What is the difference between being available for our teens and being overinvolved in their lives? What is the difference between being a controlling parent versus having a healthy level of involvement?

7. Why are chores so important for teens? What are some examples of healthy expectations for teens?

8. Think about your current schedule. In what ways would saying no to more activities help you say yes to being available?

9. As a parent, why is having your own interests and hobbies important? How can that impact your teen?

Closing Prayer

Close your time in prayer, asking for the Lord's wisdom and guidance as you parent your teen this week. Take time to rejoice in the fact that "God is our refuge and strength, an ever-present help in trouble" (Psalm 46:1).

LESSON 9

Affection:
A Home of
Warmth

GROUP DISCUSSION QUESTIONS

ICEBREAKER: What's something specific about your teen that you love? It could be a character trait, a natural ability, or something they are interested in that you enjoy.

OPENING QUESTION: Can you think of a teacher or coach who made an impact on you because you knew they loved you (not just the subject or sport)? How did they communicate their care?

1. Read Mark 12:30-31. Why is it significant that the greatest two commandments are about love? How does what we love affect how we live?

2. Read 1 John 5:2-3. How do we know whether we love God? How do we know whether we love others?

3. What observations have you made about parents who love their children more than they love God? What can you learn from the examples of Hannah and Eli? (see 1 Samuel 1–2). Why does the order of our affections matter?

4. Why can our teens be difficult to love? As parents, what does sacrificial love for our children look like? What does it not look like?

5. Read 1 Corinthians 13:4-7. How do these verses encourage you to love your teen in new ways? What phrases in this passage do you find convicting?

6. Loving our teens is not in opposition to correcting them. How can we lovingly correct rather than unkindly criticize? What's the difference?

7. What keeps you from "lighting up" when your teen walks into a room? How do you think your teen feels in your presence?

8. What does your family enjoy doing together for fun? How have you tried to create a warm environment in your home?

9. How do your teens receive love (words of affirmation, acts of service, physical touch, gifts, quality time)? Which of those is the most difficult for you to offer? Why?

10. Read 2 Timothy 3:1-17. What is hopeful about these words in the midst of a secular culture?

Closing Prayer

Spend some time in prayer together, asking God to enable you to be loving parents to your teens. Use 1 Corinthians 13 to help guide your prayers: "Love is patient and kind; love does not envy or boast; it is not arrogant or rude. It does not insist on its own way; it is not irritable or resentful; it does not rejoice at wrongdoing, but rejoices with the truth. Love bears all things, believes all things, hopes all things, endures all things. Love never ends" (verses 4-8).

Notes

1. Christian Smith and Amy Adamczyk, *Handing Down the Faith: How Parents Pass Their Religion on to the Next Generation* (New York: Oxford University Press, 2021), 5.

2. "Religious upbringing linked to better health and well-being during early adulthood," *Harvard T.H. Chan School of Public Health*, September 13, 2018, https://www.hsph.harvard.edu/news/press-releases/religious-upbringing-adult-health/.

3. I was helped with these explanations of source idols by a chart from Stephen Speaks shared on the blog of Caleb Cangelosi for Pear Orchard Presbyterian Church, PCA, https://www.pearorchard.org/notes-from-the-orchard-church-blog/2018/11/27/where-do-you-find-yourself-on-this-idolatry-chart (referenced August 13, 2022).

4. Madeline Levine, *The Price of Privilege* (New York: HarperCollins, 2006), 28.

5. Levine, *The Price of Privilege*, 33.

6. Jean M. Twenge, *iGen: Why Today's Super-Connected Kids Are Growing Up Less Rebellious, More Tolerant, Less Happy—and Completely Unprepared for Adulthood* (New York: Atria, 2017), 80.

7. Smith and Adamczyk, *Handing Down the Faith*, 225.

8. Levine, *The Price of Privilege*, 116.

9. Smith and Adamczyk, *Handing Down the Faith*, 2.

10. Tim Keller, *Prayer: Experiencing Awe and Intimacy with God* (New York: Dutton, 2014), 45.

· RAISING ·
TEENS FOR CHRIST
IN A SECULAR AGE

parenting
with hope

MELISSA B.
KRUGER

The Book That Goes with This Study Guide

Raise Your Teens on a Rock-Solid Foundation

As children mature, it's important for parents to prepare for the unique changes and challenges of adolescence. With so many cultural pressures and influences vying for teens' attention, parents need a secure foundation for creating an environment where faith can flourish.

Parenting with Hope invites you to anchor your hopes and expectations in Christ—the true source of wisdom, strength, contentment, and fruitful parenting. Integrating sound biblical teaching, insights from developmental experts, and her own experiences as a teacher and mother, Melissa Kruger will wisely guide you through today's most common concerns. Emphasizing principles over prescriptions, Melissa will help you to understand how you can build up and bless your teens in God-honoring ways.

When you recognize God as the ultimate parent, you'll begin to truly understand that he is presently at work in the hearts of both parents *and* teens. This encouraging and practical guide will equip you with the wisdom to cultivate a Christ-centered household, passing on a legacy of faithfulness to your teenage children.

To learn more about Harvest House books and
to read sample chapters, visit our website:

www.harvesthousepublishers.com

HARVEST HOUSE PUBLISHERS
EUGENE, OREGON